A **WHERE'S WALDO?** FUN FACT BOOK

FIGHTING KNIGHTS

Based on the characters created by

MARTIN HANDFORD

WRITTEN BY RACHEL WRIGHT

CANDLEWICK PRESS
CAMBRIDGE, MASSACHUSETTS

Knight Times

Knights were warriors trained to fight on horseback. They lived in Europe long ago, during a time called the Middle Ages. This lasted from about 700 to 1500. Powerful knights, who were also great lords, fought for a king or emperor. Less powerful knights might also be nobles, but fought for a great lord, instead. To pay them for their fighting, knights were often given land to live on and farm.

The most powerful people in the Middle Ages were kings and emperors. Next in line came top churchmen, great lords, and other nobles. At the bottom were poor workers called serfs. In return for a knight's protection, they farmed his land and did all the yuckiest chores.

Fighting Fashion

What a time warp! Waldo's gone back to the 1200s to help a knight get dressed! At first, knights wore armor made from linked metal rings called mail. Beneath that they wore a padded coat to soften heavy blows from enemy weapons.

Metal helmet had narrow eye slits and small breathing holes.

Cloth surcoat helped keep the sun's heat off the mail beneath.

Palms of mail mittens were made of leather, to improve the knight's grip.

Padded cap worn underneath a helmet helped soften blows to the head.

To clean off rust, mail armor was shaken in a sack containing sand and vinegar.

Padded coat acted as a shock absorber and reduced chafing from the flexible mail.

Mail stockings were tied to a belt underneath the padded coat.

Pointed spurs helped the knight make his horse gallop.

MAN IN A CAN

Mail provided protection from swords, but not from arrows or spears. So, in time, knights began covering parts of their bodies with pieces of steel called plates. Gradually, more and more plates were added.

By the 1400s, knights were covered from head to toe in plate armor. Most of the plates overlapped each other, like a lobster shell. They were joined together on the inside by straps, or by sliding or pivoting fastenings, so that the knight could bend his body.

Mail armor with steel plates, 1360.

Plate armor, 1480. With plate armor, knights no longer needed shields.

WOULD YOU BELIEVE IT, FACT FINDERS! A SUIT OF PLATE ARMOR WEIGHED ABOUT AS MUCH AS FIFTY CANS OF BEANS! BUT, BECAUSE THE WEIGHT WAS SPREAD OVER A KNIGHT'S BODY, HE COULD STILL MOVE EASILY. TALES ABOUT KNIGHTS BEING HOISTED ONTO THEIR HORSES BY CRANES JUST AREN'T TRUE!

BOLD BATTLERS

Suffering swordsmen! Waldo and Woof have stumbled across a battle! No knight worth his spurs ignored a call to arms from his king or lord — although some knights paid money instead of fighting. Big battles often began with a charge by knights on horseback. Each knight had a heavy spear, or lance, tucked under one arm, which he used to knock down the enemy. Let's hope these leading lancers don't run over our friends!

Back in the Saddle

Long stirrups and a high-backed saddle helped a knight fight without falling off his horse. Stirrups were invented in China way back in the 500s, but they didn't become popular in Europe until the early Middle Ages.

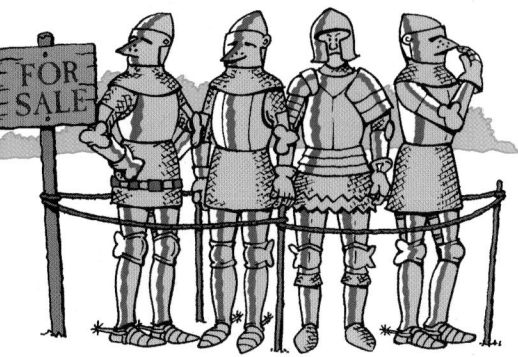

Knights for Sale

Believe it or not, knights often tried *not* to kill enemy knights in battle. Instead, defeated knights were held captive until their friends or family paid for them to be set free. A champion knight could make a lot of money if he captured the right enemy!

Wicked Weapons

After charging into battle, a knight dropped his lance and used one of his other weapons. Sometimes he fought on foot, too.

Heavy lance, 1100s
Used to knock an enemy off his horse. Light lances were used for stabbing or throwing.

Pollaxe, 1400s
Used for clobbering an enemy over the head, especially when fighting on foot.

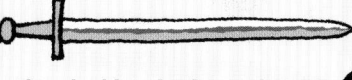

Flat, double-edged sword, 1200s
Used for slashing and slicing.

Very pointed sword, 1400s
Developed for thrusting through gaps in plate armor.

Metal-topped mace, 1400s
For clubbing and hitting while on horseback or foot.

Dagger, 1400s For close-up, hand-to-hand combat.

Good Knights, Bad Knights

During the Middle Ages a set of rules for knights was formed. These rules were known as chivalry. They were were very difficult to obey!

Rules for the Perfect Knight

1. Be a brave, daring, and skillful fighter.

2. Be a good Christian and fight all enemies of the Christian religion.

3. Think good thoughts and be polite.

4. Be kind to the poor and weak.

5. Stay loyal to your friends and don't be stingy with gifts.

6. Be a good sport in battle and treat well any knight you capture. (Remember, if you kill him, you won't be able to sell him back to his family for lots of money.)

7. Fight on behalf of a noble lady you love. Treat her with respect and do brave (and preferably dangerous) deeds to impress her.

CRUEL CRUSADERS

Many knights tried to prove they were good Christians by going on crusades. Crusades were trips to the eastern Mediterranean to fight followers of the Muslim religion. Sadly, not all crusaders behaved chivalrously. Many were horribly cruel, and used the crusades to steal and to gain great glory for themselves.

NOBLE KNIGHTS

Stories about knights and chivalry became popular during the Middle Ages. The most famous tells the legend of King Arthur and his knights. Together, they sat at a huge round table and made plans to fight bad guys. Odlaw, are you sure you're at the right table?

WARIN OF WALCOTE WAS ONE NASTY KNIGHT! WHEN TOLD HE COULDN'T MARRY THE LADY HE LOVED, HE WENT TO HER HOUSE AND KIDNAPPED HER! SEE IF YOU CAN FIND HIM SOMEWHERE IN THIS BOOK. HE HAS A SMALL STRAIGHT SCAR ON HIS FACE.

KNIGHT SCHOOL

Becoming a knight wasn't easy. By the late Middle Ages, only sons of noblemen were allowed to train for the job – which took ten years or more. All in all, it was a long and pricey process.

At about seven years old, a knight-to-be was sent to live at a relative's castle . . . without his mother or father!

There, he learned how to ride, use weapons, and behave politely. He also worked as a page, serving at dinner and doing odd jobs.

A page learned to use a lance by charging at a wooden target. He had to hit the middle of the shield on the target's crossbar . . .

without getting whacked by the sandbag on the other end. Looks like Odlaw could do with a bit more practice!

At age fourteen, a page became a squire. He would aid an experienced knight and follow him into battle.

Once a squire was eighteen or older, he was ready to be knighted. He spent the night before his knighting ceremony in church, praying.

The next day, he knelt before another knight who tapped him on the neck or shoulders with his hand or sword.

Finally, he was given his sword and spurs, which showed that he had at last become a knight.

HEY THERE, HISTORY HOUNDS! NOT EVERYONE WAS KNIGHTED IN SUCH A GRAND WAY. IN THE EARLY DAYS, SOME MEN WERE KNIGHTED ON THE BATTLEFIELD. A KNIGHT SIMPLY TAPPED A MAN ON THE SHOULDERS WITH HIS HAND OR SWORD. INCREDIBLE! HOW MANY SWORDS CAN YOU FIND ON THESE TWO PAGES?

JOLLY JOUSTS

Leaping lances! Our four friends have been invited to a joust! A joust was a competition between two knights on horseback.

WAR GAMES

Jousts often took place at fancy events called tournaments. Mock battles and fights on foot were fought at tournaments, too. Mock battles were fun fights between two teams of knights armed with lances and swords. Each knight tried to capture as many opponents as possible. The captured knights then had to pay to be set free.

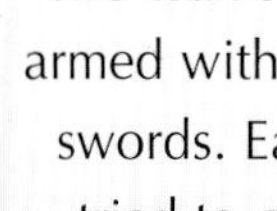

HEY, WALDO WATCHERS! DID YOU KNOW THAT A COAT OF ARMS CONTAINS NO MORE THAN 5 COLORS — BLUE, RED, GREEN, BLACK, AND PURPLE — AND 2 METALS — GOLD (YELLOW) AND SILVER (WHITE)? A STRICT RULE IS THAT A COLOR CAN NEVER BE PLACED ON TOP OF ANOTHER COLOR. CAN YOU FIND A SHIELD THAT BREAKS THIS LAW?

WILLIAM MOWBRAY

Each knight charged toward the other and tried to knock him off his horse, or to break his lance on his shield. Ladies often came to watch their favorite knight jousting. Once, a woman was even offered as a prize! Let's hope no one tries to award Wenda to the winner!

PERSONAL PATTERNS

Knights at tournaments were recognized by the colors and patterns that decorated their clothes, shields, and flags. These patterns are called "coats of arms" because knights sometimes wore them on their surcoats. Each family had its own coat of arms. When a man died, his family's coat of arms was passed on to his eldest son.

PETER, BISHOP
OF WINCHESTER

ROBERT
DE ROS

WILLIAM
LORD BOTREAUX

MICHAEL
DE LA POLE

Fun Days and Knights

When they weren't busy clobbering each other with lances and swords, noble knights loved to go hunting. The animals they caught, such as birds, boar, and deer, were tasty to eat. And galloping around the countryside was good training for war. Sometimes noble women went hunting too. Unlike men, however, they usually rode sidesaddle – with both legs on the same side of the horse. Steady on that saddle, Wenda!

Pampered pets

Knights used special breeds of dog to help them hunt down boar, wolves, and deer. Like Woof, hunting dogs were well cared for. Some even had heated kennels!

Food facts

Like other people in the Middle Ages, knights often used large pieces of stale bread as plates. After a meal, the bread was either eaten or given to the poor or the dogs. Just think how much washing up this saved!

Fun and games

In their spare time, knights liked to sing, dance, and play games such as dice and chess. Chess was often played for money, which led to arguments. It is said that King John of England once got so angry during a game of chess, he smashed the board over his opponent's head. Ouch!

 **DID YOU KNOW THAT KNIGHTS USED TRAINED FALCONS TO CATCH BIRDS, RABBITS, AND HARES? SOME OF THE FALCONS WERE SPOILED ROTTEN! THEY HAD PERCHES IN THEIR OWNERS' BEDROOMS, AND WERE FED BETTER FOOD THAN MOST POOR PEOPLE.**

HUGE HOMES

Have you ever explored a castle? In the Middle Ages a castle was a fort, house, army camp, and business center all rolled into one! It was the place where a powerful lordly knight lived with his family, servants, and soldiers. It was also where the knight's officials organized his farms, collected his rents, and judged crimes. Some castles may even have had a dreary dungeon where prisoners could be kept.

FROM STICKS TO STONES

The first castles were usually made from wood and earth. They were quick to put up but also easy to burn down, so later castles were made from stone. Early stone castles were built around a strong main tower called a keep.

Castle made from wood and earth, 1000s

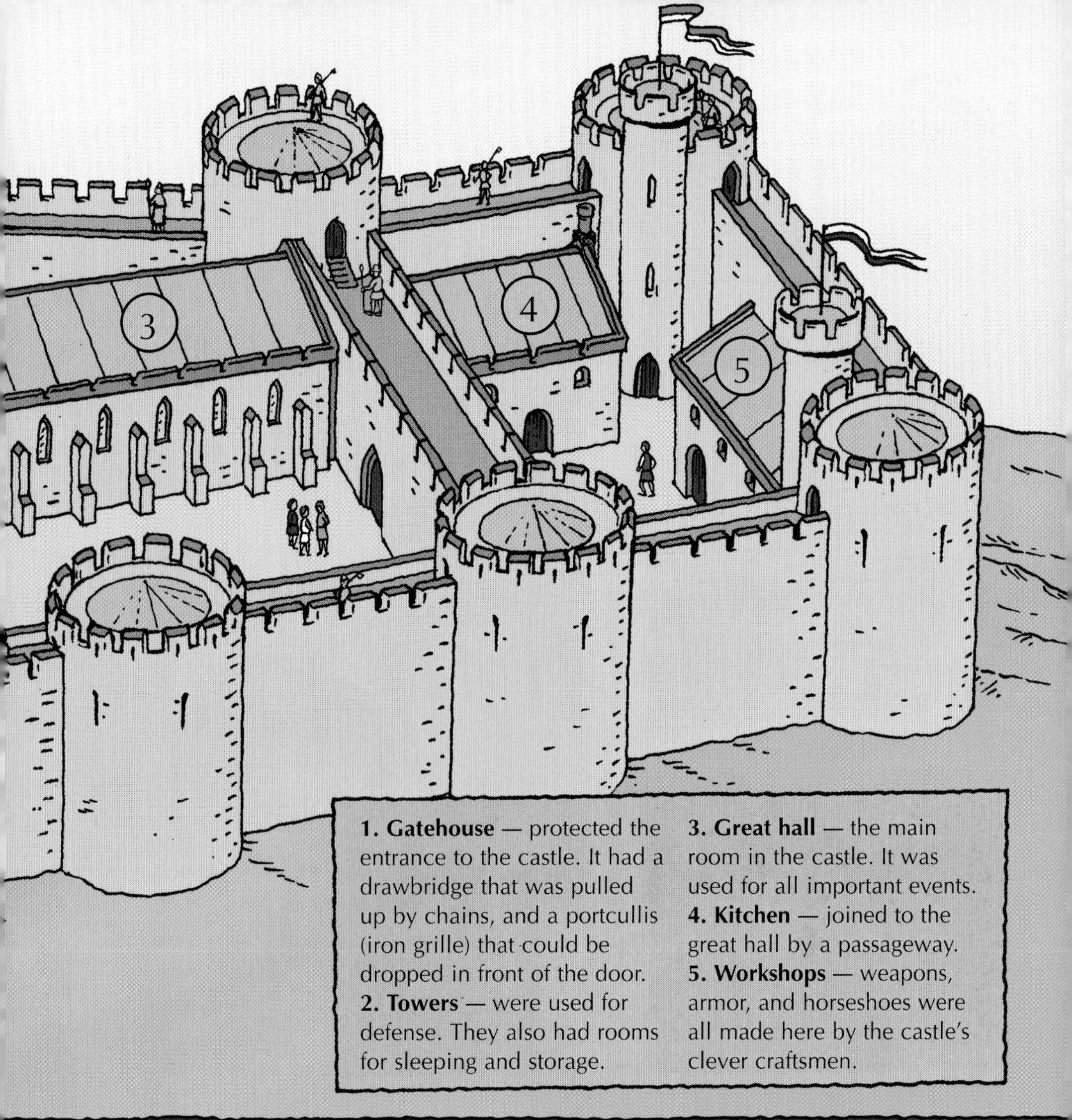

1. Gatehouse — protected the entrance to the castle. It had a drawbridge that was pulled up by chains, and a portcullis (iron grille) that could be dropped in front of the door.
2. Towers — were used for defense. They also had rooms for sleeping and storage.

3. Great hall — the main room in the castle. It was used for all important events.
4. Kitchen — joined to the great hall by a passageway.
5. Workshops — weapons, armor, and horseshoes were all made here by the castle's clever craftsmen.

Stone castle with square keep, 1100s

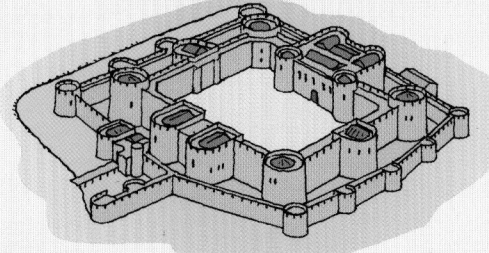

Stone castle with two circles of walls, 1200s

CASTLE INSIDES

Suffering spells! Wizard Whitebeard has made a wall of this great hall disappear! The great hall was the main room in a castle. It was used by the knights for important meetings. It was also used for eating, feasting, and sleeping. After supper, the dining tables were cleared away to make room for the many straw mattresses that the servants slept on. Only the super-rich had their own bedrooms in the Middle Ages. So, it looks like our four friends will be sleeping on the floor!

COOL FOOD

Kitchens were originally built
away from the great hall because of
the risk of fire. But food grew cold on its way
to the table, so later kitchens were built closer to
the great hall. Rooms for keeping food, baking
bread, making beer, and storing wine were also
nearby. Drinking water came from the castle's well.

ONE ROOM FEW CASTLES HAD
WAS A BATHROOM! WHEN A
KNIGHT WANTED A BATH, HIS
SERVANTS FILLED A WOODEN
TUB WITH BUCKETS OF HEATED WATER.
HOW MANY BUCKETS CAN YOU FIND
HIDDEN ON THESE TWO PAGES?

MISSION: ATTACK AND DEFEND!

Attackers used all sorts of terrible tactics to capture a castle and its lands. One popular ploy was to camp outside a castle, let no food in, and wait until the people inside starved. Another was to try to get in by force. From inside the castle, the defenders fought back furiously. They shot arrows at the attackers outside. They also hurled boiling water and rocks at them.

1. Catapults — giant slings threw huge rocks and other missiles over the castle walls.

2. Battlements — designed to hide defenders while they reloaded their weapons.

3. Arrow loops — let castle archers shoot their arrows without being seen.

4. Battering ram — its iron tip could punch holes in walls and doors.

5. Mangonel — huge slingshot powered by the tension of tightly twisted ropes.

WOBBLY WALLS

One way to break down a castle wall was to destroy it from below. Attackers dug a tunnel under the wall, propped it up with wooden posts, then set fire to the posts. The tunnel caved in, bringing down the wall with it.

GUESS WHAT, WALDO WATCHERS! CASTLES DIDN'T HAVE FLUSH TOILETS. INSTEAD, THEY HAD CHUTES THAT WERE BUILT INTO THE CASTLE'S WALLS. WASTE DROPPED DOWN THE CHUTE AND INTO A PIT OR MOAT BELOW. IN 1204 A CASTLE ATTACKER BROKE INTO A CASTLE BY CLIMBING UP ONE OF ITS CHUTES. LET'S HOPE NO ONE ELSE WAS USING IT AT THE TIME!

NIGHT NIGHT, KNIGHTS!

As the Middle Ages went on, the way wars were fought changed. Rulers began hiring more and more soldiers who fought for money, not for land. And foot soldiers armed with pikes, crossbows, and guns became more powerful in battle than knights with lances. Slowly but surely, the days of the knights came to an end.

STICKY BUSINESS

By the late Middle Ages, foot soldiers were the most important part of an army. Some carried pikes — a kind of spear about twenty feet long. A "hedgehog" of pikemen could severely wound a charge of knights.

FEEBLE FIRE

Gunpowder was first used in Europe in the 1300s, and knights in armor were no match for it. For starters, guns loaded with gunpowder were as unreliable as Odlaw. Sometimes they even blew up in the marksman's face! In time, however, they became much more reliable . . . and much more deadly.

THE END OF CASTLES

Like knights, castles slowly fell out of fashion. This was partly because private wars between castle owners became less common, so fortlike homes were no longer needed. Also, when gunpowder and cannons became powerful, castles were no longer safe. Nowadays, all that is left of many castles are their lonely ruins.

THE FIGHTING KNIGHTS CHECKLISTS

CALLING ALL WHERE'S WALDO? TIME-TRAVELERS! NOW THAT YOU CAN TELL A LETHAL LANCE FROM A DEADLY DAGGER, GALLOP BACK TO THE BEGINNING OF THE BOOK AND START SEARCHING FOR ALL OF THESE KNIGHT-TIME THINGS.

KNIGHT'S CHECKLIST

- [ ] Four fallen spurs
- [ ] Sixteen fluttering flags
- [ ] A closed book
- [ ] A lost horseshoe
- [ ] Nine striped tents
- [ ] Two mighty maces
- [ ] A scary skull
- [ ] An open book
- [ ] A lazy mouse
- [ ] A broken wine barrel
- [ ] Sixteen horses
- [ ] A brown briefcase
- [ ] Five gray shaggy dogs
- [ ] A knight picking his nose
- [ ] Three men with shovels

LOST PROPERTY

Can you remember where you first spied these knightly knick-knacks?

FEUDAL FEATURES

All these faces appear in the book, but not exactly as they look here. Can you find the differences?

ANSWERS

Good Knights, Bad Knights — Warin turns up in *Fun Days and Knights*.
Knight School — Nineteen steely swords and two wooden ones.
Jolly Jousts — Odlaw's shield in *Knight School* breaks this law.
Castle Insides — Three buckets.

First U.S. edition 2001
Library of Congress Cataloging-in-Publication Data is available.
Library of Congress Catalog Card Number 00-030406
ISBN 0-7636-1301-0
1 2 3 4 5 6 7 8 9 10
This book was typeset in Optima.
The illustrations were done in ink and colored electronically.
Printed in Hong Kong

Candlewick Press
2067 Massachusetts Avenue
Cambridge, Massachusetts 02140